Cudjo's Own Story

of the

Last African Slaver

Zora Neale Hurston

Martino Fine Books
Eastford, CT
2020

Martino Fine Books
P.O. Box 913,
Eastford, CT 06242 USA

ISBN   978-1-68422-478-4

Copyright 2020
Martino Fine Books

Cover Design Tiziana Matarazzo

Printed in the United States of America On 100% Acid-Free Paper

Cudjo's Own Story

of the

Last African Slaver

Zora Neale Hurston

The University of Chicago Press on behalf of the Association
for the Study of African American Life and History
1927

Originally Published in *The Journal of Negro History*,
Oct., 1927, Vol. 12, No. 4 (Oct., 1927), pp. 648-663.

CUDJO'S OWN STORY OF THE LAST AFRICAN SLAVER [1]

About four miles above Mobile, at the mouth of the Chickasabogue Creek (now called Three Mile Creek), on red clay bluffs, on the Old Telegraph Road, but now reached by the new Bay Bridge Road and Craft Highway, is African Town. The site was once and still is to a large extent the possession of the Meaher Brothers, Tim, Lim and Burns; these men had a mill and shipyard at the mouth of the creek and built vessels for blockade running, river trade and filibustering expeditions.

The three Meaher brothers were natives of Maine. They had associated with them in business one Captain Foster, born of English parentage in Nova Scotia. He was the actual owner of the *Clotilde*. She was selected because of her fleetness to make the voyage for a cargo of slaves.

Once on the African Coast, there was little trouble in procuring a cargo of slaves; for it had long been a part of the trader's policy to instigate the tribes against each other and in this manner keep the markets stocked. News of the trade was often published in the papers. An excerpt from *The Mobile Register* of Nov. 9, 1858, said: "From the West Coast of Africa we have advice dated Sept. 21st. The quarreling of the tribes on Sierra Leone River rendered the aspect of things very unsatisfactory. The King of Dahomey was driving a brisk trade in slaves at from fifty to sixty dollars apiece at Whydah. Immense numbers of Negroes were collected along the Coast for export." Fos-

[1] This story was secured by Miss Zora Neale Hurston, an investigator of the Association for the Study of Negro Life and History. She made a special trip to Mobile to interview Cudjo Lewis, the only survivor of this last cargo. She made some use, too, of the *Voyage of Clotilde* and other records of the Mobile Historical Society.

ter, with a crew of Northern men, sailed directly for Whydah.

The slaves who made up the cargo of the *Clotilde* were captured by Dahomey's warriors and women warriors (perhaps Amazons), Cudjo, or more accurately, Kujjo Lewis says in this manner. In the early part of the nineteenth century one of the Dahomey kings organized a battalion of women warriors.

For a long time the King of Dahomey and his tribe had been raiding the weaker and more peaceful tribes that lay within striking distance of his empire. They lived by war and slavery. The King of Dahomey's house was built of skulls. They made war upon Togo.

Togo was "many days from the water." About fourteen, Cudjo estimated.[2] The people of the Togo were a peaceful, agricultural people, raising hogs, goats, sheep, chickens, and a few cows. They planted corn, beans and yams. Plenty of bananas and pineapples grow wild. The most important natural resource was the palm tree. They produced palm oil, their greatest industry. They made cord for all purposes by twisting strips of palm leaves. They made cloth from the fibre, and beer from the nuts. The men and women tilled the fields alike and held property in common. There was no hunger, no poverty.

Their methods of farming are interesting. A plot of ground is tilled by the tenant for seven years. By that time the fertility is about exhausted and they choose another plot. The yams are produced from the eye of the seed as we do our white potatoes. The vines grow very long, so they are poled like string beans. The earth is hilled up about the shoot and the weeds kept away until it gets a start. "Then," says Cudjo, "we go way, we come back, push, dig de dirt—great beeg yam like keg, nail keg. We cut off vine with little piece of yam and cover it up again. Another beeg yam. Whole family couldnt eat at one time. For seven years don't need no new seed, it keep making yams."

[2] According to some accounts these slaves were brought from Loanda.

A sort of melon grows on tall plants and is eaten with salt as one does cantaloupe, but it grows very much larger. It is without doubt the melon tree found everywhere in the tropics, probably of the papaya family. Beer is also made from bananas and is used as commonly as the "vin rouge" of France.

Foods are roasted and boiled. The roasting and boiling is done over and among the coals, but the boiling is done over the fire in clay pots. There is a definite fire place—built in. Three clay pillars or pot-rests about eighteen inches high are molded of clay and allowed to dry. The fire is built among these posts and the pot rested on them.

The drinking of milk is unknown to them. They eat almost no domesticated beef. They eat goat flesh, chicken, hogs, deer, and other game, as they are great hunters. Elephants are hunted for ivory, but the flesh is never eaten. This is a staple however with cannibal tribes. Hogs are prepared by taking brown sage and burning off the hair, then washing the skin thoroughly. The animal is usually roasted whole very much as we barbecue. This was probably the origin of the barbecue in America. The word, however, is derived from a native name in Guiana.

The houses of these Africans are cylindrical and built of clay. They are thus weather-tight and fireproof. A circular trench is dug and the walls built up about two feet high and eighteen inches thick. This is left to dry. Then they add another two feet and let it dry. This is kept up until the house is about eight feet high. A series of notches are made at the top to receive the rafters. The center pole is a tall, straight palm tree. Slight niches are cut in this to receive the rafters, one end is laid through the notches at the top of the wall, and the other fitted into the niches in the center pole and bound with palm cord. The ends in the notches are bound and cemented with clay. When this dries it is very strong and durable. Then the roof is laid with grass. A kind of long leafy grass like wheat stalks is used, the rafters having been grilled over with young saplings bound with palm cord. The grass is bound on the lower edges of the roof first and the next course overlaps this as ordinary shingles are laid to shed water until the entire roof is covered. A very watertight roof results.

Openings of the house are limited. There are no windows. The door is made by boring holes in one set of timbers and fitting tongues or wooden pegs on the transverse pieces. These are fitted carefully and when driven together interlock like the "dovetailing" in antique furniture. There are no hinges. The door is set up or moved away as convenient. The floors are of beaten clay. The house is lighted by a palm oil lamp. The niches for these lamps are left in the thickness of the wall.

The apparel is also interesting. The men wear a pair of short trousers ordinarily, but on special occasions this is supplemented by a cloak. A large piece of cloth about six feet square is first draped over the left shoulder. The short end from the back folds smartly over the other end, thus holding it in place, and giving a very pleasing effect and at the same time leaving the right arm free. Plenty of jewelry is worn, earrings of ivory and bracelets of gold and ivory.

The women wear a single garment, also a square of cloth. Nothing is worn above the waist but ornaments. Bracelets from wrist to elbow and numerous shell and ivory necklaces—as many as the husband can afford. Earrings and bracelets of pure gold that tinkled very pleasantly as the women swung their arms, Cudjo says.

The cloth is always of cotton woven by men. The colors are bought from men, not quite as white as white men— who go and sell, probably the Arabs. On a large flat stone are little troughs gouged out of the rock to hold the different colors and the weaver takes from each when he chooses. Shoes are made of cowhide but they consist of the merest sandals. Buffalo hide is also popular.

There was a military organization but they were not a

very warlike nation. All boys over fourteen were of military age. The people of Cudjo's native country fought largely in self defense.

The natives are polygamous but the wives never exceed three or four. There is no jealousy among the wives for another wife merely lightens the duties of the first. She herself does the match-making for her successors and holds the most favored position. The wives are always bought of their parents, but no presents are made to girls before betrothal. A native is careful not to give anything until he is sure he has the bird in hand.

"Cudjo he been married for three years for example," says he. "His wife says: 'Cudjo, I am growing old. I am tired—I will bring you another wife.' Before speaking thus she has already one in mind—some girl who attracts her and whom Cudjo has possibly never seen. The wife goes out and finds the girl—maybe in the public square, maybe in the market place and she asks: 'You know Cudjo?' The girl answers: ' I have heard of him.' The wife says: 'Cudjo is good. He is kind. I would like you to be his wife.' The girl answers: 'Come with me to my parents.' They go together; questions are asked on both sides and if they are satisfied the parents say: 'We give our daughter into your care. She is ours no more. You be good to her.' "

The wife returns with the girl to Cudjo's house. The wife introduces the girl to Cudjo, shows her how to look after things as she has done, then sits down to take her days of rest and ease, and works no more. Marriages are contracted with surrounding friendly tribes. The bride is always taken to the home of the groom. A woman belongs to her husband's tribe.

The relation of the husband to the wives is that of a protector. He dares not commit adultery for the punishment is very great. If the wife is caught in adultery she is returned to her parents and her purchase price must be returned to the husband. The status of a divorced woman is a great deal lower than that of the married woman, since for one thing and only one thing she is divorced. Her former husband however is not spiteful. Her people refund and he feels satisfied. He has lost nothing.

There is very little of illegitimacy. When it does occur, the man is forced to pay her parents dowry, since he has been the cause of their not getting one from a prospective husband; and the child is brought up by his people. The girl is disposed of for a smaller consideration, probably to some much less desirable husband.

The boys are circumcised at seven or eight years and on the fifth day after circumcision, when the soreness has passed, the boys are given a feast. This marks the passing of an important stage in their preparation for life. They march about the village and beat drums all day.

Drums are made in three shapes. The small tom-tom, the large state drum, and the long drum covered at both ends. Deer and buffalo hides are used for covering. These drums are used for religious and festive purposes.

With respect to birth Cudjo thinks there probably were such ceremonies, but he has no memory of them. There was no puberty ceremony as in most tribes. Cudjo would have gone through them if there had been, for he was past nineteen when he came to America.

These natives are religious. "Alahna" is the great god of all. Women make sacrifices to him to grant them children if they are barren. There are other gods whom the natives worshipped. They had a dualistic belief in spirits. There was a spirit of Good, "Ahla-Ahra." Spirit of evil Ahla-hady-oleelay." The priest was called "Elaha." They were what we call pagans, nature-worshippers of the wind, the sun, thunder and lightning. They knelt in fear before these powers with their arms crossed over their breasts. Cudjo frequently employs this gesture. Cudjo is now an ardent Christian and is, I believe, hiding or suppressing what he knows about African religion for fear of being thought a heathen.

If Cudjo is a good example of his native stock they are a tall, well-built tribe of people, dark brown but by no means black. They have a very well-developed forehead and back head and intelligent eyes. The hair is Negroid but less so than many American Negroes. Cudjo's feet are small for his height. Cudjo is keen, intelligent, cheerful. He has a lively imagination and a fine sense of humor. He has a radiant smile. At the age of about ninety he still has all of his teeth but three.

Cudjo mentions certain tribal marks. The teeth are cut so that the two front ones come to a point at the center, the others so as to make a broad inverted "V" on either side. There is no other mark, but I am told by old citizens of Mobile that some had two lines between the eyes and three on the cheek, which led me to conjecture that when Captain Foster was selecting the Negroes on the African coast he mixed them. Cudjo later explained that the teeth are the marks of family and of kinship but that the lines are tribal. They might have all come from the same general locality and might have spoken the same language.

The people of Cudjo's tribe were ruled by a king called "Adbaku" or "Ibaku." The country was rather democratic. Any one might see the king. He regularly presided over the court of justice. One of the severest tribal laws was against theft. Such a crime was almost unknown. Houses were never locked. Everyone worked and had plenty.

"Suppose," says Cudjo, "I leave my purse. You know the square in Mobile? I talk, I go way and leave my purse on de ground. Every body see it. They say: 'Cudjo forget his purse.' Nobody steal it. When I get to de Creek (Three Mile Creek) I feel I see I left it on de square. I say its too far to turn back. Today I have no time. I get it tomorrow. Tomorrow I am too busy again, but it stay there. Nobody move it because it belongs to Cudjo. Could I do that in America?"

Murder in Cudjo's tribe is always punished by death. Just the way the victim was put to death so the murderer would be executed. All are equal before the law. Rank and wealth count for nothing. There is a regular building set aside for the king to hear cases; but, as a rule, court is held in the public square.

While living in their peaceful state there came serious trouble from without. The arrogant King of Dahomey sent to the King of the Togo and, according to Cudjo, said: " 'You have corn and yams, and cattle, you must give me half.' He lived like at Montgomery, the Togo live like Mobile—One sleep away about 200 miles. The King says: 'No, you have hands you make corn and yams and fruit for yourself.' The King at Dahomey he was very mad because we send message like that so he say: 'We make war on the people of Togo.' But he be afraid. One traitor from Togo, he wants big honors in the army so he goes to King of Dahomey and say: 'I show you how to take Togo.' All night they march. Some go on one side. They hide, lay low down in de woods. Others go on other side, they lay low in de woods. All around they go. Some come in, but they say when they git inside: 'Don't make no noise.' " (The ambush was to keep hidden until they heard the slaughter begin. Then they were to intercept the fleeing.) "Oh Loi! Oh Loi!" said Cudjo thus telling the story and crossing his arms upon his bosom.

The village was surrounded at daybreak with great slaughter. The surprised village was helpless before the cruel forces of Dahomey. The women warriors perpetrated the most awful butchery. Some of the men when attacked were already in the field working to get their work done before the heat of the day. They were butchered without quarter. Not one escaped. The invaders fell upon the sleeping women and children. All were either killed or captured. Dahomey's women warriors overpowered and bound the most stalwart men. The women in their paint and dress looked like men. The victors cut off the heads of the dead, leaving the bodies where they had fallen. The heads were taken home as evidence of individual valor and as trophies to be hung on the huts at Dahomey. Cudjo's face still registers horror when he tells of this awful experience.

On their march to the Coast, they were forced to behold the dangling heads of their relatives and friends. When they grew offensive, the Dahomans stopped the march that they might smoke the heads. As they passed near one of Dahomey's villages at a curve in the big road, they caught sight of fresh heads raised on poles above the huts. With the captives there were some of other tribes, friends who had been visiting in the raided village. The towns they passed through on their march to the sea were "Eko," "Budigree" (Badraejy?), "Adache" and Whydah. At Whydah was a white house on the river bank, behind this was a stockade in which they were held about three weeks, at which time Captain Bill Foster came.

Captain Foster left Mobile secretly and made a good voyage until he was near Cape Verde Islands. A hurricane struck him and he had to put in there for repairs. The Northern crew of the *Clotilde* mutinied for more pay and threatened to inform the officials of the purpose of his voyage. Foster hurriedly promised more pay without the slightest intent of keeping his word. His wife in relating this incident remarked that the Captain had always said that promises were like pie crust—made to be broken. He made friends with the Portuguese officials by gifts of shawls and sailed away when repairs were made and anchored safely in the Gulf of Guinea where he had to anchor more than a mile from shore and be taken to land in a small boat.

On shore, he was taken by six stalwart blacks to the presence of a prince of Dahomey, a great, stout black weighing over three hundred pounds. This prince was hospitable and showed Foster the sights of Whydah, one of which was a large square filled with thousands of snakes kept for religious ceremonies. Wishing to make a present to Foster, this prince asked him to select a native, one that the "Superior wisdom and exalted taste" of Foster designated the finest specimen. Gumpa was his choice. Foster made this selection with the intention of flattering the Prince to whom Gumpa was closely related. This accounts for one member of Dahomey's tribe in "African Town." He became known as African Peter. He used to tell his story in a sentence: "My people sold me and your people bought me."

When Captain Foster went to the stockade where the captives were imprisoned they were placed in circles composed of ten men or ten women, Foster standing in the middle. Says Cudjo: "He looked and looked and looked. Then he pointed to one and then to another." Foster thus selected one hundred and thirty after which he got into the hammock and was conveyed across the river to the beach. Behind him marched the captives chained one behind the other. They had to wade, the water coming up to their necks.

They wore clothes made of cotton but as they stepped into the small boats which were to take them to the *Clotilde* the Dahomans avariciously tore their garments from them. Men and women alike were left entirely nude. This is still a great humiliation to Cudjo. He regards as great injustice the accusations of some of the American Negroes that they were naked.

The captives were put into the hold of the *Clotilde*. In this respect the *Clotilde* was better equipped than most slavers. The usual space in which the "Middle Passage" was made was from two and a half to three feet in height, and the miserable captives were stowed away very much as sardines are packed in tins without even room to sit up. The hold of the *Clotilde* was deep enough to permit the men of lesser stature to stand erect.

When one hundred and sixteen had been brought aboard, Foster went up into the rigging with his glasses to look about the harbor. He said that all of Dahomey's vessels were flying black flags. He hurried down and gave orders to leave all slaves who were not yet aboard, to weigh anchor, and to get immediately under way. The treacherous

Dahomans dealt also in piracy, and were making ready to head down upon the *Clotilde*, recapture the slaves and take Foster and crew prisoners. She made her escape, likewise evading an English cruiser.

At the end of the thirteenth day the Africans were removed from their close, dark quarters. Their limbs were so cramped and numbed they refused to obey their wills, so they were supported by some of the crew and walked about the deck until the use of their limbs returned. Says Cudjo: "We looked and looked and looked and we saw nothing but water. When we come from (which direction) we do not know, whar we go, we do not know." One day they saw islands.

Cudjo says that on the twentieth day Foster seemed uneasy, that he climbed the mast and looked with glasses for a long time. Then he came hurriedly down, ordered the sails down, threw out the anchors, and ordered the Africans back into the hole. Thus the ship lay until night. The captives were close observers. During the voyage they seem to have been very alert. They noted the varying colors of the sea.

Foster was kind to them, though they were fed very sparingly and only a little water was given them twice a day. "Oh Loi! Oh Loi!" says Cudjo, "we so thirst! Dey gib us leetle beeta water twelve hours. Oh Loi! Oh Loi!" The water tasted sour (of vinegar, not putrid).

When the *Clotilde* sailed into American waters, they were put back into the hold. Three days before they landed when the *Clotilde* lay waiting behind the islands in the Mississippi Sound and near the lower end of Mobile Bay, a bunch of green boughs was brought to them to show that the voyage was almost at an end.

To make the hiding more secure, the *Clotilde* was dismasted. Then Foster got into a small boat rowed by four sailors to go to the western shore of Mobile Bay, intending to send word to Meaher that the *Clotilde* had arrived. His approach was regarded with suspicion by some men ashore and he was fired upon. Waving a white handkerchief, he allayed their doubts, and he offered fifty dollars for a conveyance which would take him to Mobile.

Captain Foster reached Mobile on a Sunday morning in August, 1859, his return from the Slave Coast being made in seventy days. Arrangements had long been made that a tug should lie in readiness to go at a moment's notice down Mobile Bay to tow the *Clotilde* and her cargo to safety. When the news came, the pilot of the tug was attending service at St. John's Church. Captain Jim Meaher and James Dennison, a Negro slave, hurried to the church. The three hastened down to the wharf and were soon aboard the tug. They waited for darkness to approach the *Clotilde*. It was made fast and the trip up the bay was begun. *The last slave ship was at the end of its voyage.*

The tug avoided the Mobile River channel, slipped behind the light house on Battery Gladden, into Spanish River. As the *Clotilde* passed opposite Mobile the clock in the old Spanish tower struck eleven, and the watchman's voice floated over the city and across the marshes: "Eleven o'clock and all is well."

The *Clotilde* was taken directly to Twelve Mile Island, a lonely place. There waited the *R. B. Taney,* named for Chief Justice Taney of Dred Scott decision fame. Some say the *June.* Lights were smothered and in the darkness, quickly and quietly the captives were transferred to the steamboat and taken up the Alabama River to John Dabney's plantation below Mount Vernon. They were landed the next day.

At Twelve Mile Island, the crew of Northern sailors again mutinied. Captain Foster, with a six shooter in each hand, went among them, discharged them and ordered them to "hit the grit and never be seen in Southern waters again." They were placed aboard the tug. Meaher bought tickets and saw that they be put on a train for the North.

The *Clotilde* was scuttled and fired. Captain Foster himself placed seven cords of light wood upon her. Her hull lay in the Marsh of Bayou Corne, and could be seen for many years. It is now below water. Foster afterwards regretted her destruction as she was worth more than the ten Africans given him by the Meahers as his booty.

The Africans were kept at Dabney's place for eleven days, being only allowed to talk in whispers, and constantly moved from place to place. At the end of the eleventh day, clothes were brought to them, and they were put on board the steamer *Commodore* and carried to the Bend in Clark County where the Alabama and the Tombigbee rivers meet and where Burns Meaher had a plantation. On the Dabney plantation they had been left in the charge of the slave James Dennison who later married Kanko, one of their number, and became a resident of "African Town." On the Burns Meaher place they were lodged each night under a wagon shed, and driven each morning before daybreak back into the swamp where they remained until dark.

Meaher sent word secretly to those disposed to buy. They were piloted to the place of concealment by James Dennison. The Africans were placed in two long rows, the women on one side, the men on the other. Some with tears streaming down their faces and shouting "Ele, Ele! Home, Home!" (?) were sold and sent to Selma. Of this band until recently a man and woman still lived. Captain Meaher took thirty-two slaves, sixteen men and sixteen women, Captain Burns Meaher ten, five of each, Captain Bill Foster ten, Captain Jim Meaher about eight. Finally Captain Tim Meaher put them to work. "We astonish to see de mule behind de plow to pull," said Cudjo.

The Africans, however, would stand for no mistreatment. "Once an overseer attempted something which the women considered as such and he was overpowered by them and given a sound thrashing."

After war was declared there was no danger of exposure and the Africans belonging to all mentioned above were taken to the Meaher settlement at Magazine Point where they were kindly treated by their respective owners. Burns Meaher alone kept his and they told of great hardships; but after the close of the Civil War, these joined the others at Magazine Point.

The part they settled became known as "African Town." The name Plateau was bestowed when the Mobile and Birmingham (now Southern Railway) came through. The town of Plateau, with Magazine Point, has two thousand inhabitants. It is not incorporated. It has no Mayor, although one Murray, the store keeper, is referred to as such. The Meaher heirs still hold a large part of the real estate and all of the mill sites. There is no pavement of any kind. The settlement is not lighted.

The slave experience prepared the Africans for what came thereafter. They were able to manage crops and make a living. The men went to work at a dollar a day in the mills and the women made and marketed the produce. They seem to have been very industrious, for most of them became home owners.

After emancipation, these Africans wished to go back to their own country, but they had no means. They concluded to save and said to their wives: "Now we want to go home and it takes a lot of money. You must help us save. You see fine clothes—You must not crave them." The wives promised and answered: "You see fine clothes and new hats —now don't you crave them either. We will work together." They found that they could save almost nothing. They talked among themselves of how Meaher had brought them from their native land and how now they had neither home nor country. Cudjo was always the spokesman. He would present their case to Meaher.

Soon after he was cutting timber just back of where the schoolhouse now stands, Captain Tim Meaher came along and sat upon a felled tree. Cudjo saw his opportunity and stopped work, all his emotions in his face.

The Captain looked up from the stick he was whittling and asked: "Cudjo, what makes you so sad?"

"I grieve for my home," said Cudjo.

"But you got a good home."

"Captain Tim, how big is Mobile?"

"I dont know, I've never been to the four corners, Cudjo."

"If you give Cudjo all Mobile, that railroad, and the banks of Mobile, Cudjo does not want them, for this is not home."

Cudjo in relating this breaks down in tears, saying "Oh Loi! Oh Loi!"

"Captain Tim, you brought us from our country where we had land and home. You made us slaves. Now we are free, without country, land or home. Why dont you give us a piece of this land and let us build ourselves an African Town?"

"Fool! Do you think I will give you property upon property? You do not belong to me now!"

So they all bought property from Meaher, who made them no concessions. They worked and saved, living on molasses and corn bread or mush. Their African home faded as each year bound them closer to America. They became farmers, and Cudjo still makes his living this way.

Having no head of the tribe and understanding that in a country of different institutions a king would look ridiculous, they selected Gumpa, African Peter and Jaybee as judges to preside over the colony. When disagreements came up, word would be sent each member that there would be a meeting at a certain place after dark, their only leisure time, possibly at the home of one of the judges. The offender would be given a hearing before the whole group. The first time the criminal would be reprimanded; if he again offended, a whipping was administered by one of the judges.

When the Africans were set free, all days were alike. But some American Negroes came to them and led them into the Church and all became ardent Christians. Cudjo is most devout. They built first "The African Church." It is now called the "Old Land Mark Baptist Church" with Rev. Mr. Keeby as pastor.

The last eight of the one hundred and sixteen Africans were: Abache (Clara Turner), Monachee (Kitty Cooper),

Shamber, Kanko (who married Jim Dennison), Zooma (of Togo Tribe), Polute, Cudjo, and Orsey, or Orsta Keeby. Cudjo is the only one alive at present, a dignified, lovable, intelligent man.

Cudjo says he wishes at times to return to his native land, but he realizes that he would be a stranger there. He doubts even if he could locate the graves of his relatives. All that he is sure of is here, the graves of his wife Albine and all of his children. He has numerous descendants. He is glad that he was brought to America, since here he found the true God. He is very vigorous though he is nearing the century mark.

Cudjo likes to tell Old Testament stories and Samson is his favorite. He is fond of making what he calls parables. He made one about his wife's death. He places his head in his hands and "lifts it up" to speak his "parable." Cudjo lifted his head and spoke this:

I will make a parable. Cudjo and Albine have gone to Mobile together. They get on the train to go home and sit side by side. The conductor comes along and says to Cudjo: "Where are you going to get off?" and Cudjo answers: "Mount Vernon."

The conductor then asks Albine: "Where are you going to get off?" and she replies: "Plateau."

Mount Vernon is several miles beyond Plateau.

Cudjo is surprised. He turns to Albine and asks: "Why, Albine! How is this? Why do you say you are going to get off at Plateau?"

She answers: "I must get off." The train stops and Albine gets off. Cudjo stays on. He is alone. But old Cudjo has not reached Mount Vernon yet. He is still journeying on."

He made another parable about his wife. He lifted up his head and said:

I will make a parable. "Suppose you come to my house and want to go to Keeby's. You have an umbrella and you leave it in my care. When you come back you ask for your umbrella. Must I give it to you or keep it?" "No, Cudjo, you cannot keep it. It belongs to me. It is not yours." Triumphantly Cudjo concludes: "Neither could I keep Albine; she was just left in my care."

ZORA NEALE HURSTON

Notes

Made in United States
Orlando, FL
14 February 2024

43659299R00017